**Journey**Through®

Job

40 Daily Insights by **Christopher Ash**

Design by Joshua Tan
Typeset by Lidya Jap

ISBN,978-1-913135-56-0

Printed in the United Kingdom
21 22 23 24 25 / 5 4 3 2 1

Foreword

Do good things happen to good people? Can I expect bad things to happen to bad people? Do I live in a moral universe? Is good behaviour rewarded, and will evil be punished? It matters; it matters a lot. It matters because it is not easy to be good. If I am to try to be good, I would like to be sure that it will pay to be good. And, perhaps, I would want bad things to happen to bad people (so long as I can avoid being one of them).

It matters when bad things happen to me or to someone I love. Suppose we are living the life of faith, seeking to follow Christ; what, then, if things go terribly wrong for us? Does that mean we have missed some key to blessing? That we are hiding some secret sin? What else might it mean?

It also matters when good things happen to bad people. Why do they happen, when they so clearly don't deserve it?

It matters when you feel the misery of a messed-up world. Is there any hope? Does Christ make any difference? He does! He really does. And Job will show us how. As you read through Job, ask yourself the following questions:
1. How does Job help me understand and feel deeply the innocent sufferings of Jesus Christ?
2. How does Job open my eyes to the true character of God and warn me about distorted ideas of God? (This is especially important when my judgment is distorted by my sufferings.)
3. What insights does Job give me into what a follower of Jesus might expect to experience in life?

Christopher Ash

We're glad you've decided to join us on a journey into a deeper relationship with Jesus Christ!

The *Journey Through* series is designed to help believers spend time with God in His Word, book by book. Each title is written by faithful Bible teachers to help you read, reflect and apply God's Word, a little bit at a time. It's a great accompaniment to read alongside the Bible, digging deeper into God's Word. We trust the meditation on God's Word will draw you into a closer relationship with Him through our Lord and Saviour, Jesus Christ.

How to use this resource

READ: After reading and reflecting on the Bible verses, use the explanatory notes to help you understand the Scriptures in fresh ways.

REFLECT: Use the questions to consider how you could respond to God and His Word, letting Him change you from the inside out.

RECORD: Jot down your thoughts and responses in the space provided to keep a diary of your journey with the Lord.

Think about the character of the leaders in your country or region. What are the marks of their greatness? Is their greatness accompanied by true goodness?

Think of some of the best people you know who genuinely love God and trust in Christ. What has been their experience of life? Would a modern equivalent of Job 1:1–3 be true for them?

Day 2

Read Job 1:6–2:10

When the world is in the middle of bewildering changes—a big shift in global power, even a war—we wonder what is going on behind the scenes—really behind the scenes, in heaven itself. What is God doing in all this? We do not know, but we would like to. For if we knew what God was doing, we could truly understand our world.

In today's passage, we read two "behind the scenes" parts (Job 1:6–12 and 2:1–6) and two events on earth (1:13–22 and 2:7–10). Try reading the events on earth on their own. You'll read of a good and great man suffering the bankruptcy of his great business and the bereavement of all his children, and then, the loss of his health.

On the face of it, this is caused by a toxic mixture of what we might call terrorism (the Sabeans and the Chaldeans) and what we loosely call natural disasters (although they are not really natural). The big question—and it is a very big question—is: *Why* did these things happen? And why to such a good man?

That question opens up the wider questions of why bad things happen to genuine, God-fearing people. In the end, it makes us ask: Why did the supremely good man Jesus die by crucifixion?

Now read behind the scenes. Here we meet the Lord, who is the Sovereign God in complete control of His world. He is governing His world through a sort of Cabinet meeting of angels (1:6; 2:1), who are more powerful than humans but less powerful than God. Among these is one called Satan, which means adversary or enemy.

The Bible teaches that God is in complete control; and yet He exercises His control through intermediary powers, some of whom are evil. **God is not evil, but in His infinite wisdom and power, He uses evil to work His purposes of good.**

Astonishingly, Satan has a job in God's government. It is a strange but vital job. He must determine whether someone who looks like a worshipper of God is a genuine worshipper. And he does it by taking away their blessings.

Only when our blessings are taken away, will it be seen if we genuinely worship God because He is God. The prosperity-gospel worshipper is a false worshipper. Satan asks to test Job, and the Lord says he may. In some deep way, it is necessary for the glory of God that Job should suffer and be proved genuine.

ThinkThrough

Look carefully at Satan's argument in Job 1:9–11. Why is prosperity no proof of our genuineness as worshippers? How has testing in your life revealed what is in your heart?

Meditate on Job's responses (1:20–21 and 2:10). How do they reveal the heart of a genuine worshipper?

Day 3

Read Job 2:11–3:26

Job's three friends represent the wisdom of the world. They come with the best of motives, to "sympathise with him and comfort him" (Job 2:11). But they fail. They say nothing to him for seven days, which is the traditional response when mourning for a corpse (see 1 Samuel 31:13). They cannot "recognise" Job or get through to him. He is deeply alone.

Job is so alone that in chapter 3 we hear him voice a dark lament that is addressed neither to his friends nor even to God. He doesn't speak it *to* anybody; it is just squeezed out of him by his misery. He curses the day of his birth (Job 3:3–5) and the night of his conception (vv. 6–10), wishing he had never come to be. Hope is darkened. "Leviathan" (v. 8) is a storybook monster that vividly portrays a supernatural power of evil; we shall meet him again in chapter 41, where he seems to be a picture of Satan himself.

In 3:11 and 16, Job asks that desperate question: "Why?" If only he had died at birth (v. 11) or been stillborn (v. 16), then he could have lain down at peace and been at rest (v. 13); instead, he now has to live in a world where the wicked cause him endless distress and trouble (v. 17), and his life is like a captive never at ease (v. 18).

Somehow, Job cannot simply lie down under his sufferings. **He must begin—as now indeed he does begin—a painful journey of honest faith.** It is this journey that drives the remainder of the book and leads to a conclusion full of gospel hope.

In verses 20 to 26, Job broadens his lament to include not just himself in his own suffering, but also the seemingly pointless suffering of "those in misery . . . the bitter of soul" (v. 20). Again he asks the question, "Why?" (vv. 20, 23). And again he speaks of "no peace, no quietness . . . no rest, but only turmoil" (v. 26).

It is important to try to feel the misery of Job. In chapters 1 and 2, we watched, as observers, the trials of Job; in today's reading, however, we enter the inner world of the misery of Job's soul.

It ought to be both poignant and painful for us to hear these words. They help us enter the agony of Jesus Christ as He lived and died under the wrath of God, paying the penalty for sinners. For the darkness of Job anticipates, again and again, the darkness of the cross of Christ.

ThinkThrough

Read Job 3 aloud, slowly and with feeling. Try to enter the feelings of Job in all their intense darkness. Meditate on how this agony anticipates the sufferings of Jesus Christ.

Have you, or others dear to you, ever experienced any echo of how Job feels here? Take time to praise God that this is not the end of the story. It is not the end of Job's story, it was not the end of Jesus' story, and it will not be the end of your story, or that of any believer.

Day 4

Read Job 4:1–5:7

In the movie *The Sound of Music*, when the handsome Captain von Trapp declares his love for Maria, the young heroine sings a song that perfectly expresses the worldview of Job's comforters. Trying to work out why something so good should have happened to her, she sings, "Somewhere in my youth or childhood I must have done something good."

I am experiencing blessing, so I must have done something good to deserve it—Job's comforters would agree with this statement, and they apply this same logic to his situation, in reverse: "You are experiencing suffering, so you *must* have done something bad."

From chapter 4 through to 26, Job and his three comforters take turns to make speeches, with Eliphaz starting in chapter 4. It is clear from chapter 3 that Job is deeply distressed, and Eliphaz begins fairly gently (Job 4:2–6). He reminds Job that he has been a wise counsellor to others and encourages him to take his own medicine now.

"Job," he says, "you know the moral framework of the universe. You know that bad things happen only to bad people and good things to good people. So, you need to think about your own life."

Verses 7 to 11 are important. In verse 7, Eliphaz reminds Job that they all know that innocent people never perish. Never! When people behave like aggressive lions, God punishes them (vv. 10–11).

In verses 12–21, Eliphaz describes a strange, mystical dream or vision. The content of this vision is that mortal human beings cannot expect to be righteous in the presence of God. We need to remember our frail mortality and not get ideas above our station as mortals. This is an implicit rebuke to Job.

The rebuke becomes more explicit in 5:1–7. "What's the point," says Eliphaz, "of all your resentful crying out (vv. 1–2)? It's just how fools behave (v. 3), and you have seen what happens to fools (vv. 3–7)!" Eliphaz is not impressed with Job's misery. He thinks Job needs to "man up", face the facts, and not get so agitated about his sufferings. After all, he must have done something to deserve it.

In 42:7, the Lord's headline verdict on Eliphaz, Bildad, and Zophar is that they have not spoken rightly about Him. So, we need to ask where Eliphaz goes wrong. Much of what he says is true. But, he makes at least one big mistake. Job 4:7 sums it up: **There is such a thing as**

undeserved suffering, and the cross of Christ is the supreme example!

Job himself is a true believer. His sins are covered by the sacrifice of Christ, even though that sacrifice will not happen till many centuries later. Job does not deserve what he is suffering, and Eliphaz is wrong to imply that he does.

When sitting with a Christian who is suffering, have you ever spoken to them like Eliphaz?

Have you ever wondered if they might really deserve what is happening to them? Repent and meditate on the reality of undeserved suffering for the believer.

Read Job 5:8–27

A friend of mine was reading the latest book by atheist Richard Dawkins, which is aimed at teenagers. Dawkins writes with great confidence. He sounds impressive and gives the impression that he knows a lot. But my friend, a scholar in an ancient field called Assyriology, realised that a section of the book was chock-full of factual mistakes. It sounded impressive, but it was actually plain wrong, again and again!

Eliphaz ends his first speech with a very confident assertion: "We" —Eliphaz and his friends—"have examined this, and it is true. So hear it and apply it to yourself" (Job 5:27). Eliphaz brings the weight of his and his friends' shared conviction to what he says. We have "examined" it; we know it is "true". But is it?

In this closing section of Eliphaz's first speech, Eliphaz tells Job what he would do if he were in Job's place. He says Job should "appeal to God"—so far so good!—because God helps humble people (vv. 8–16). So, if you are humble, you may have a chance of God helping you. But—and here is another rebuke from Eliphaz to Job— God "thwarts the plans of the crafty . . . catches the wise in their craftiness" (vv. 12–13). You are trying to be too clever, Job, by puzzling out these big questions about your suffering. Just lie down before God and be humble.

Now the strange thing about this is that Paul actually quotes something Eliphaz says—"He catches the wise in their craftiness"—in 1 Corinthians 3:19. It's true: God does catch the wise in their craftiness. So, what's the problem? **The problem is that Job is not being crafty; he is being honest. He is a deeply humble believer.**

But then Eliphaz goes on (Job 5:17–26) with a beautiful appeal to "the discipline of the Almighty" (v. 17). The passage sounds quite like Hebrews 12:4–13. It has lovely imagery and reads as an attractive appeal. Accept this discipline, Job, and you may expect God to restore you and bless you. God is correcting you (v. 17), and I am sure you need correction!

What's wrong with Eliphaz's statements? We need to be reminded of what we have been told three times, once by the writer and twice by God, that Job is already a blameless, upright, God-fearing, and repentant believer (Job 1:1, 8; 2:3). Eliphaz is speaking to the wrong man.

Ultimately, we can see the mistake of Eliphaz most clearly if we imagine him saying these things to the Lord Jesus Christ, accusing Him of being "crafty", exhorting Him to humble himself under God's discipline, and so on. Eliphaz is confident, but wrong.

ThinkThrough

Think about the words "if I were you" (Job 5:8). How often have you assumed you know what is going on in the heart of another believer, and given advice on the basis of what you assume to be true? Repent and resolve to listen more and be more careful.

Consider if there have been times when you have asserted things with more confidence than is justified. Resolve to be more careful.

Day 6

Read Job 6

Why are you making such a fuss over your food? This is how parents chide their children who cry rather than eat a perfectly good meal. There's nothing wrong with your food, they say, so why are you crying? This is a trivial example, but we shall see that it is close to the illustration Job himself uses to show the difference between him and his comforters (Job 6:5–7).

Job's first speech runs through chapters 6 and 7. Chapter 6 seems to be addressed to his three friends, whereas chapter 7 is spoken to the Almighty God. Eliphaz has asked Job why he is making such a fuss about things (see 4:2, 5; 5:2). That may seem strange, given the depth of Job's sufferings. And yet the depth of Job's lament in chapter 3 goes beyond the sadness of a man bankrupted, bereaved, and sick; it is a lament against *God*.

Eliphaz doesn't think Job should do this. But Job insists that if his "anguish could be weighed and all my misery placed on the scales", it "would surely outweigh the sand of the seas" (6:2–3). Verse 4 shows why it is so unbearably bad. It is not simply that it hurts; it is that it comes from God! The Almighty God has fired poisoned arrows into Job, and it terrifies him.

In verses 5–7, Job uses an illustration similar to the one I gave earlier: a wild animal doesn't make a fuss when it has decent grass or fodder, but the diet I have been given is utterly disgusting! I am not making a fuss about nothing; I am troubled because it is right to be distressed when experiencing the wrath of God. (By his diet, Job may mean the wrath of God or the useless words of his friends.)

Job is so desperate that in verses 8–13, he wishes God would kill him while he is still able to be patient and not deny God. He feels very weak, but he doesn't want to deny God, for he is a real believer.

From verses 14 to 21, he compares his friends to a *wadi* or stream bed in the desert hills. A caravan of desert travellers turns aside to find water in this *wadi*, but when they get there, they find it is bone dry, and they perish. Job's friends are like that: he has turned to them for words of hope, but they have nothing. The reason they have nothing is that there is no good news in what they say, no message that will bring help or comfort to a sufferer. They "have proved to be of no help" (v. 21).

Job hasn't asked his friends for money or military help; he just wants to hear words that will enable him to understand and bear up under his pain (vv. 22–23). But they have nothing—no gospel, no hope, just the empty words of human morality and religion. It's just "good things to good people" and "bad things to bad people"; that "system" has no gospel, for there is then no possibility of guilty people being blessed—which is the gospel!

Do you have the experience of not being able to help a fellow believer who is suffering? Or of speaking words that do no good? It's hard. Ask yourself: Were my words of morality, or were they of the gospel, the true gospel?

Job longs for simple kindness (Job 6:28). Is there a suffering believer to whom you can show simple kindness today?

Day 7

Read Job 7

Go away! Go away! I long to be with you, but when I am with you, life is so miserable that I would really rather you went completely away! That's a sad conversation, but not unfamiliar between lovers. Angry words like these are sometimes heard between parents and teenagers.

If Job has been complaining to his friends in chapter 6, he now speaks directly to the God whom he loves, and yet whose presence has become unbearable to him. It is one of Job's many poignant speeches in the book.

Job 7:1–10 laments over the apparent pointlessness of Job's life, and the life of others in a similar predicament. It is like "hard service" (v. 1), which means something like slave labour (see 1 Kings 5:13–14). The nights seem to go on so long, month after month seems utterly futile, and a day dawns with a hint of hope but is soon gone, and it is back to night again (Job 7:2–6). Job feels he will never be happy again. Before long he will be dead, buried, and completely forgotten; his life will have counted for nothing. He will have left no mark on human affairs (vv. 7–10).

From verses 11 to 21, Job cries out to the God whom he loves and longs for. But it is such a paradox. His sufferings under the wrath of God are so deep that he actually voices the wish to be forsaken by Him (vv. 16, 19).

Like a girl challenging her boyfriend to go away, Job wishes God would leave him alone. He is full of "anguish" and "bitterness of . . . soul" (v. 11). God seems to think Job is "the sea, or the monster of the deep" (v. 12, that is, a hostile creature like Leviathan) and must be put under close guard. God won't leave him alone, even at night, but sends terrible nightmares (v. 14). "Let me alone," cries Job (v. 16).

Verse 17 sounds like Psalm 8 with its question, "What is man?" But where Psalm 8 answers that men and women are entrusted with great honour by God, Job asks why God keeps such a hostile watch over him (Job 7:18–21). Why can't He just leave him alone?

Job 7 helps us understand the terrible burden of bearing the wrath of God. **In his undeserved sufferings, Job foreshadows the later climactic sufferings of Jesus Christ as He bears the wrath of God against sinners.** This is what it feels like. It is far worse than bankruptcy, than bereavement, than the loss of health; for it is the displeasure of God from whom alone we draw hope for life.

Read Job 7 aloud and take time to *feel* the depth of Job's misery. Then meditate on the infinite weight of suffering borne by the Lord Jesus as He carried the wrath of God for us.

Remember that the believer today must expect some overflow of this suffering (see Colossians 1:24). Meditate on this, praying especially for believers whom you know are suffering today.

Day 8

Read Job 8

He is a Christian. He lives an upright life, as far as we can see. All was well with him until last week, when his wife and son were killed in an accident. What do you say to him? What do you say if you believe there is a just God who is in control of the world?

Bildad gives us one answer. Listen carefully to it, because it looks as if it should be true. Bildad is speaking to an upright man (Job 1:1), to whom a series of terrible things has happened. Job says he doesn't deserve it, but Bildad says he does. In Job 8:2–4, Bildad asserts that God would never do anything unjust. It follows that when Job's children died, they deserved it (v. 4).

So, what is Job to do? In verses 5–7, Bildad appeals to him, in beautiful words, that if he seeks God and lives an "upright" life (v. 6), then all will go well with him again.

Bildad is sure that only good things happen to good people; if bad things happen, it proves that someone is bad. If Job doubts this, he should listen to verses 8–19. Here, Bildad insists that what he teaches has been known for a long time (vv. 8–10). In nature, there is a simple law: water leads to growth, and no water leads to no growth (vv. 11–12). In the same way, goodness leads to blessing, and badness to curse. This is why people who forget God have such a hard time (vv. 13–19). Even if things go well with them, they won't last.

In verses 20–22, Bildad ends his appeal with the conclusion: if Job is really blameless, then God will give him laughter, joy, and victory. His message is simple and clear: "Job, you must have deserved these bad things that have happened to you. God is always fair. So you need to plead urgently with God and try to be good and upright (which you obviously haven't been), and then hope that things will get better again.

What should we make of Job's friends? Are they right or wrong, good or bad, or a mixture? Job 42:7 is a key verse that will help us work this out. God says they didn't speak correctly! Even if some of what they say may be right (and it is), the big message is badly wrong. So, we need to ask about Bildad (as about Eliphaz and Zophar): What was wrong with what he said?

What do you think is wrong with what Bildad says?

Some of what Bildad says is right, although it doesn't apply to Job. What do you think he gets right? How can you avoid becoming a "Bildad"?

Day 9

Read Job 9

I have never lived through an earthquake. Those who have will testify that it is a terrible experience. We assume solid ground is just that—solid—and that when we walk on it, we know where we stand. But when an earthquake strikes, to our horror, solid ground shakes. Job is living through a kind of moral or religious earthquake, and it shakes his convictions about God.

Job used to believe just what Bildad believes (as do Eliphaz and Zophar). "Indeed, I know that it is true," he begins (Job 9:2). Job has believed that good things happen to good people, and bad things to bad people. But now, he is beginning to doubt it: "But how can . . ." (v. 2).
Job is beginning to honestly question what he had previously believed.

What matters most to Job is to be in a right relationship with God (v. 2). But how can he do this? God is so strong (vv. 3–4), and—this is the problem— He is shaking the earth (vv. 5–6). There is a moral earthquake: bad things are happening to a good person, and Job cannot understand it. His friends assume his sufferings must mean he is secretly a bad person, but Job knows (as do we, the readers) that this is not true (see 1:1, 8; 2:3). God is simply too strong for Job: He is invisible and invincible to Job (9:11–13). Job longs to talk to God, to reason with Him, and to ask Him to answer his question, "Why?" But God will not listen (vv. 14–20).

And then, in a moment of extraordinary daring, Job simply accuses God of being unjust. In verses 21–24, he says God "destroys both the blameless"—like Job—"and the wicked". As far as Job can see, when there are unjust judges, it must be God who causes them to be unjust. For "If it is not he, then who is it?" (v. 24).

Job doesn't know what to do about this. Maybe he should just forget about the problem and smile anyway (v. 27); perhaps he should try harder to be good (vv. 30–31). But neither of these will work. Or—and this is a great insight—maybe, just maybe, he could find "someone to mediate between us" (v. 33), to bring him into God's presence that he might speak with Him without fear (v. 35). That longing for a mediator is a seed thought that will bear gospel fruit later.

Be honest. When you look around at the world (and perhaps at your own life), do you sometimes find yourself wanting to agree with Job that if there is a sovereign God, He must be unjust?

Meditate on how Job describes the awesome power of God. Compare this to your own instinctual ideas which may be weaker. Be sobered as you think about the sheer greatness and overwhelming power of God.

Read Job 10

Have you ever been to the funeral of a stillborn child? As you look at the tiny casket, do you wonder why God went to all the trouble of weaving this intricate little human being together in his or her mother's womb, only for him or her to die without doing anything—without speaking, smiling, or loving? It is a sad thought that brings tears to our eyes.

For Job, his life now feels much like the life of that child. **As Job grapples with the strange sovereignty of God and the deeply puzzling way in which God governs the world, he asks four questions in great agony.**

First, in Job 10:1–3, he asks why God is so determined to be against him. "Tell me," he says to God, "what charges you have against me" (v. 2). Job feels like a prisoner condemned without a proper trial, without even being charged. And while God seems pleased to oppress Job, He smiles on the plans of the wicked (v. 3)! If Job is right, there is no justice in the universe.

Job then asks God if He can see straight (vv. 4–7). He knows that mortals, who are with "eyes of flesh" (v. 4), cannot see right. But if God can see right, why, when He knows Job is not guilty, does He insist on continuing to search out Job's faults?

In verses 8–17, Job describes in beautiful poetry the care with which God has taken in creating Job. God's hands shaped and made him (v. 8), moulded him as a skilled potter with clay (v. 9), shaped him just as an expert cheese-maker would turn milk into cheese (v. 10), clothed him with skin and all the parts of his body (v. 11), knit him together in his mother's womb (v. 11; see also Psalm 139), gave him life (Job 10:12), and watched over him through birth and his life, up until his troubles (v. 12).

But why did God do this? Was God simply doing it to enjoy the sadistic pleasure of destroying him, and turning him back to dust to make sure he was punished even for the sins that had been confessed, repented of, and forgiven (v. 14)? To Job, God is like a relentless military foe bringing wave upon wave of forces against him, to destroy him utterly (v. 17).

Why then, Job asks finally (vv. 18–22), does God not simply kill him? Job might as well have been like a stillborn child, "carried straight from the womb to the grave" (v. 19); he might as well have gone "to the land of gloom and utter darkness" (v. 21). There is an echo here of Job's lament in chapter 3.

Consider the *apparent* pointlessness of the earthly life of Jesus. Why should God make such a good man, then allow Him to be killed with such cruelty? How might you answer someone who asked you this question?

Think about a believer you know who feels his life is pointless, or who is in such a dark place that he cannot see why life is worth living. How might it encourage them to know that Job has been where they are, and that God dealt kindly with Job in the end?

Day 11

Zophar is the third and final friend to make a speech in this first cycle of speeches. His words expose the cruelty of any religious system of morals that is devoid of the gospel.

When human morality, religion, or philosophy asserts the simple truth that good things will always happen to good people and bad things to bad people, what follows? **Not only do the prosperous become self-righteous, supposing that their happiness is a reward for their virtue; but also when a believer suffers, he is told that his suffering *must be* a punishment for his sins.**

Zophar is very blunt with Job. In Job 11:2–4, he expresses his anger. He thinks Job is an empty talker. When Job claims to be right with God (v. 4), this must be nonsense; so Zophar will answer Job as he deserves (v. 2). We are likely to agree with Zophar. But we need to remember that three times we have been most emphatically told that Job is a genuinely blameless and upright man who worships God and repents from evil (Job 1:1, 8; 2:3). Job is in the right with God, and Zophar is wrong.

But Zophar goes further. In 11:5–6, he says he wishes that God would show

Job that "God has even forgotten some of your sin." That is to say, your sufferings are less than you really deserve. It is not enough that you lose your property, your children, and your health; you deserve worse than that!

In verses 7–9, Zophar praises the infinite wonders of God, and rightly so. But—and here is the problem—in verses 10–12, he makes it clear that he, Zophar, understands that God in His wisdom has put Job in prison because He recognises that Job is a deceiver and a stupid man. Not only is Zophar saying that Job is guilty, but he is also implying that he, Zophar, can understand the limitless wisdom of God. Neither claim is true.

In verses 13–20, Zophar makes Job what appears to be a generous offer on behalf of God. If Job will repent of his sin (v. 14), then God will bless him abundantly. But if he won't, there is no hope for him (v. 20).

So there is a double problem here. On the one hand, Zophar does not actually understand what is happening. Not at all. Reread the heavenly scenes in Job 1 and 2; Zophar has no clue! On the other hand, Zophar is accusing Job of being a secret and impenitent sinner, when he is not. Human religion is both arrogant and cruel.

ThinkThrough

Ask yourself if you have ever spoken in a way that implies that you know what is going on in someone's heart, and how he or she stands before God. Repent and resolve not to do so again.

Reread Job 11:7–9 and bow before God in His limitless majesty (as Zophar fails to do).

Read Job 12:1–13:19

Who can refute a sneer? This was the question William Paley, a famous Christian of an earlier century, asked. He was referring to a clever book in which Christianity was not argued against, but rather laughed at as absurd. It can feel excruciating to be laughed at. Job's friends, who were initially horrified at his predicament, have reached the point where they are actually laughing at the absurdity of Job's speeches. For them, the world is very simple and they find it extraordinary that Job cannot see it.

In today's reading (Job 12:1–13:19), he speaks to his friends. In 13:20–14:22, he speaks to God.

In 12:2–6, Job accuses his friends of laughing at him (v. 4). They are so arrogant; they think they are the people who really understand things. So they look down their noses at Job in his misfortune.

In verses 7–12, Job mimics what his friends have said to him. They are saying that their system is so simple that even animals, birds, the earth, or fish can understand it. They are the senior people whose long life has given them good understanding (v. 12). "So," they are saying, "why won't you listen to us? Everybody else—even the fish!—knows this is true." But what Job's friends are saying is shallow. In a mocking tone, Job says that if the fish can understand it, then perhaps there is more to the world than this!

In the next section (vv. 13–25), Job looks around at the world as it is. What he sees is a lot more complicated than "good things happen to good people and bad things happen to bad people". He speaks of what we call natural disasters, when things are torn down, when there is drought, when God sends floods (vv. 13–15). These things do not fit into a simple system.

In verses 16–21, Job looks at disasters that happen to different people—rulers, judges, priests, trusted advisers, elders, nobles, and the mighty. If they trusted in Job's friends' simple system, some of them would be in for a terrible shock.

The world is more complicated than that—a lot more complicated. Nations go up and down (v. 23) and leaders can go mad (v. 24). The world is a wild place. **Job wants to face this head-on, and not pretend that a simple moral system explains it all.**

In 13:1–12, he accuses his friends of telling lies about God. Job wants to speak directly to God himself (v. 3) and resolves to do so; he knows it is dangerous ("Though he slay me", v. 15), but he must do it.

ThinkThrough

Do we as Christians ever give the impression that the world is simpler than it is? Meditate on the puzzles of the world and resolve to speak more carefully.

Think about Job's determination to speak with God himself. Pray that you will develop the same yearning, and not simply to speak with others about the things of God.

Day 13

Read Job 13:20–14:22

It is sad to watch a tree being cut down. And yet, sometimes, the tree will sprout again from the stump and there is new life. How much sadder to watch a human being die and be buried. For you know there is no equivalent to "sprouting again" with new life. When they are dead, they are dead. We even use the expression "dead and buried" to speak of a final end. It is this that Job dreads.

After speaking to his friends (Job 12:1–13:19), Job now takes his life in his hands and speaks with great faith-filled perceptiveness to God himself. He has said, "I desire to speak to the Almighty and to argue my case with God" (13:3), and now he does. He begins by asking God to give him an intermission in his sufferings, possibly so that he can concentrate (v. 21); he also asks God to summon him to speak (v. 22). Job knows that he cannot just walk into the presence of God, but needs to be given permission.

Job proceeds to describe what he wants to say to God. There is an insightful sequence here. Job begins by lamenting the problem of sin (vv. 23–27). He is deeply aware of his sins. He knows that when God hides His face, when God blows him around like a dry leaf or harvest chaff, when God punishes him—all this is to do with sin. **Job repents habitually, but he knows the burden of sin. His sufferings foreshadow the Lord Jesus who will also bear the burden of sins, the sins of many for whom He will die.**

It is natural that Job should move from sin to mortality (13:28–14:6). He feels deeply that his life, indeed human life in general, is like fruit that goes rotten or a piece of clothing eaten by moths (13:28); that life is short and troubled (14:1); and that human beings are like short-lived flowers or fading shadows (v. 2). All this is because we are sinners in a world under sin. (Even for the Christian, "your body is subject to death because of sin"—Romans 8:10.)

Then, Job moves from mortality to the finality of death itself (Job 14:7–12). He brings home this terrible finality by comparing life with a cut-down tree. It is this final end that Job dreads. But, most wonderfully, he then yearns for bodily resurrection (vv. 13–22), without which there can be no hope. In a deeply personal passage, he expresses hope for that day when God will call to Job in his grave and Job will answer. And Job will be ransomed, healed, restored, forgiven!

Job hopes for the bodily resurrection that will later be brought to light in the gospel. Meditate on the shortness of our human lives and treasure this hope.

Consider how the prospect of bodily resurrection gives hope to suffering believers.

Day 14

Read Job 15

I was speaking with a Christian woman who was going through some terrible suffering. "What have I done wrong?" she asked. "I must have done something wrong and God must be punishing me." Job's comforters would have agreed with her. "Yes," they would have said, "you must have. And now you need to repent."

In this second of Eliphaz's speeches, he has dropped the kind tone that ran through much of his first speech (Job 4 and 5). In 15:1–16, he is very angry with Job. At the heart of his anger is the accusation that Job's words "undermine piety and hinder devotion to God" (v. 4).

Let us explore this. How would Job's words stop people from worshipping God as they ought? Answer (and this is the answer of all religions without the gospel): if we break the connection between virtue and reward, and between sin and punishment, then there is no incentive left to be good. Why be good, why fear God, if it doesn't necessarily lead to blessing? Why not be bad, if you may not be punished for it? This is the objection that people made to the gospel of grace when Paul preached it many years later: "Let us do evil that good may result" (Romans 3:8).

In Job 15:17–35, Eliphaz paints for Job a vivid picture of what happens to the wicked. As he does so, we cannot avoid the conclusion that the man whose picture he is painting looks and feels very much like Job himself! This man is tormented by terrible fears (vv. 20–24), just as Job is. He challenges God (vv. 25–26), just as Job is doing. His riches end in bankruptcy (vv. 27–29), just like Job. He will die before his time (v. 32), much as Job looks like may be doing.

The conclusion is obvious: if this is what happens to the wicked man, and this is what is happening to Job, then Job must be this wicked man! You must have done something terribly wrong, Job. If only you would admit it, repent, turn back, and seek God, then you might be restored.

How wrong Eliphaz is! Job is not sinless. But he is blameless, upright, God-fearing, and repentant. **He is not suffering because he has sinned.**

Do you find yourself agreeing with Eliphaz's speech to Job? Most of us do at times. Consider how easy it is to abandon the gospel of grace (the forgiveness of sins given to us in Jesus and foreshadowed in the Old Testament), and go terribly wrong.

Think about undeserved suffering (above all, the cross of Christ) and undeserved blessing. Consider that the Christian should expect to experience both undeserved blessing (what we call grace) and undeserved sufferings—the overflow of the sufferings of Christ (see Romans 8:17). Do you expect both in your life of discipleship?

Day 15

Read Job 16:1–21

I don't watch violent movies. And yet, reading the Bible can feel like that sometimes. The way Job describes being violently attacked by God is horrifying. But we need to hear it if we are to understand the sufferings of Christ and the trials of believers.

In Job 16:2–5, Job says two remarkable things. First, he calls his friends "miserable comforters" (v. 2) —they come to bring comfort but actually make him more miserable! Job's friends have no gospel of grace. Second, and very surprisingly, he says that if they were suffering, he would actually comfort and encourage these same friends (v. 5). When someone is a real believer, they not only long for God's comfort, but also yearn to bring that comfort to others (see 2 Corinthians 1:4).

In Job 16:7–14, Job tells us what it feels like to be under the wrath of God. **As we read these words, we should meditate on their ultimate fulfilment in the sufferings of Jesus Christ.**

Job's deepest suffering is not his bankruptcy, nor the loss of his children, nor even the disintegration of his own health, but the hostility of God. For Job cares more about God than anything else. What hurts most is not just that he is worn out, that his household has been devastated, and that he himself is now all shrivelled up and gaunt, but it is also that God has done all these things (vv. 7–8). God has attacked him in a deeply personal and desperately violent way (v. 9). Socially, this means that Job has been handed over to wicked people who jeer and scorn him (vv. 10–11). God is like a cruel army general leading His troops against Job in wave after wave of violent attack (vv. 12–14).

Job is sure he is innocent (v. 17). In verses 18–21, he voices an extraordinary cry of faith. Echoing the blood of righteous Abel crying out from the ground for justice (Genesis 4:10), he cries to God for a "witness" in heaven who will intercede for him, who will mediate (see Job 9:33). This witness must be God (for no other witness would have sufficient authority) and must intercede with God. The fulfilment of Job's longing must wait until Jesus Christ comes as that Mediator.

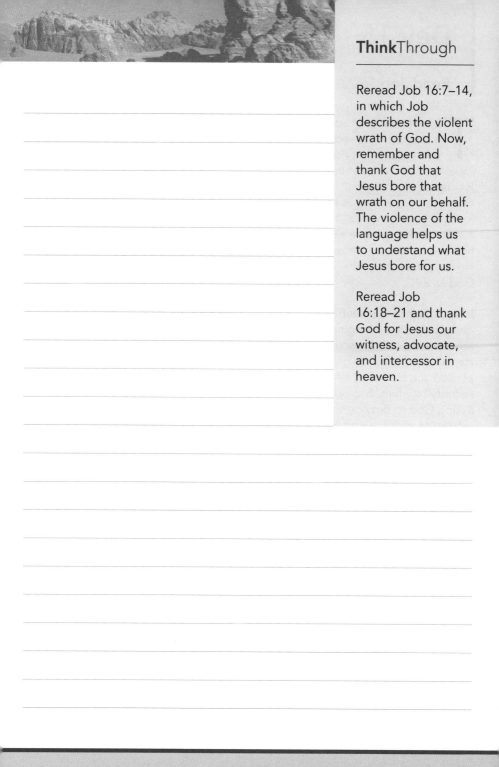

ThinkThrough

Reread Job 16:7–14, in which Job describes the violent wrath of God. Now, remember and thank God that Jesus bore that wrath on our behalf. The violence of the language helps us to understand what Jesus bore for us.

Reread Job 16:18–21 and thank God for Jesus our witness, advocate, and intercessor in heaven.

Day 16

The remainder of Job's speech is very dark indeed. Death is everywhere. Very soon he will "take the path of no return" (Job 16:22). He has no more "spirit", no more desire for life; all he has to look forward to is the grave (17:1). He is surrounded by people who look on him and mock him, because they see him as a man under the judgment of God (v. 2).

In verse 3, however, Job seems to come back to the longing for an advocate or intercessor (see 16:18–21). He calls upon God to give him "the pledge you demand" or to "put up security" for him. Job seems to be asking God to provide some kind of substitute sacrifice who will pay the penalty for his sins, who will satisfy the wrath of God against him, and who will die in his place.

Job's circumstances are dark indeed. **If people want a well-known example of what it is to be under God's judgment, Job is an easy man to choose; he is a byword for this.** People spit at him (17:6), and his "eyes"—which in biblical language speak of desire or the love of life—"have grown dim" as his spirit fails with all his sadness (v. 7). His "whole frame"—his bones, muscles, sinews, and the whole of his body—"is but a shadow" just fading away (v. 7). He is an appalling sight.

In verse 10, Job challenges his friends to keep on attacking him, for he has nothing to lose. He has no more life to lead, no more plans to make, no more desires in his heart (v. 11). All he can look forward to is the grave (v. 13). The place where his body will rot ("corruption . . . the worm") will be to him like a strange pair of parents, his mum and dad (v. 14). As he laments in chapter 3, all is dark as his hope goes with him "down to the gates of death" (v. 16).

This is a haunting foreshadow of the sufferings of Christ as He bears the wrath of God for us (2 Corinthians 5:21; Psalm 22:1).

Read Job 16:22–17:16 again slowly, meditating on the sufferings of Job and then the sufferings of Jesus Christ. Thank God for His love in sending Jesus to do this for you, and thank Jesus who "loved me and gave himself for me" so personally (Galatians 2:20).

Is there a believer facing death with whom you can sit and pray, and whom you can encourage that Jesus has gone this way before? If so, go and sit with them.

Day 17

Read Job 18

My wife and I do not watch horror movies, as they would give us nightmares. Our imaginations are too vivid. But, to listen to this speech of Bildad is not far from the experience of a horror movie. Except that the sufferings that Bildad describes are real; no actor or actress is pretending here. Bildad is describing hell.

Bildad begins his speech, as the other friends often do, by telling Job how annoying he finds him (Job 18:1–4). But then he says something that puzzles us: "Is the earth to be abandoned for your sake? Or must the rocks be moved from their place?" (v. 4)

In the Bible, the solid rock, or earth, is a picture of the stability of the world. It speaks of a place of order (in contrast to the chaotic seas), a world in which there is a definite right and wrong. Bildad assumes this must mean that bad things happen only to bad people. He thinks that Job, in protesting that he is not bad, is asking for an exception to be made to the moral structure of the universe; Bildad thinks this is outrageous!

In the rest of his speech (vv. 5–21), Bildad teaches Job about the "place" of the wicked. It is a frightening description, but the significant thing to note is that every bit of this description also describes Job's current situation!

This place is very dark (vv. 5–6), as Job's life is now (see 17:13). The wicked are brought here like a trapped animal when God the hunter ensnares and captures them (18:7–10), just as God has hunted or stalked Job (10:16). This place is very frightening (18:11–14), a place where "terrors startle" and a man is "marched off to the king of terrors", just as Job is terrified by God (9:34). It is what happens when people disappear from this world of life and hope forever (18:15–20). This, concludes Bildad, most certainly "is the dwelling of an evil man . . . the place of one who does not know God" (v. 21).

Job needs to draw his own conclusions. If his experience of suffering matches this description of what happens to people who don't know God, then he must be such a person. Job needs to repent quickly if he is to have any hope. This is the message of Bildad.

Bildad's description of hell is frighteningly accurate; it is all true. The problem is that Job is blameless and upright, a man who fears God and turns from evil (1:1, 8; 2:3).

Job is suffering the terrors of hell even though he does not deserve it!

ThinkThrough

When Jesus suffered, people thought He must have been under the judgment of God. They were right. But the sins for which He suffered were ours, not His. Job is a picture for us of these sufferings of Jesus. Meditate on how Jesus endured hell for us.

Feel the terrors of hell as Bildad describes them. Then, pray for your unsaved family members, colleagues, and neighbours.

Day 18

Read Job 19

Many of us have experienced the thrill of listening to Handel's *Messiah*, with its wonderful words, "I know that my Redeemer liveth", followed by, "And now is Christ risen from the dead" (from 1 Corinthians 15). And rightly so. Today, we hear the first of those sayings as Job speaks of them many centuries before Christ.

Bildad has accused Job (implicitly) of being a man under the righteous judgment of God. Job now agrees that he is under the judgment of God—but challenges the accusation that he deserves it. His friends have used his "humiliation against (him)" (Job 19:5); that is to say, they have deduced from Job's humiliation that he must be an impenitent sinner.

In verses 1–12, Job describes his experiences as if God had mugged him in the street. "Violence!", he cries out, but no one listens or helps (v. 7). God tears him down and attacks him with wave after wave of His troops.

In verses 13–20, Job moves from the focus on God as his attacker to the misery of how his sufferings have isolated him. Family, friends, servants, and even his wife have abandoned him. This is an echo of the loneliness of hell. In verses 21–22, he cries out for his friends to have pity on him because God is pursuing him.

Then, his tone changes. In verses 23–24, Job longs that someone would write down his defence in permanent form, so that no one can erase it. He wants the world to know he is innocent. In an astonishing clarity of faith, he says: "I know that my redeemer lives" (v. 25).

This redeemer can be none other than God himself. **Somehow, Job knows that God will stand for him, as it were, against the wrath of God.** And he will see Him (vv. 25–27).

God the Father did this for the innocent Jesus: He vindicated Him, as we know from the resurrection ("But Christ has indeed been raised from the dead", 1 Corinthians 15:20). And God will redeem all who belong to Jesus.

Job concludes with a word of warning to his friends (Job 19:28–29). They need to remember that there will be judgment. When Job is vindicated, they will be condemned, unless they repent of the wrong way they are treating him (see 42:7–9).

ThinkThrough

Meditate on the loneliness of Job (Job 19:13–20) and how it must have felt. Then, consider the loneliness of Jesus Christ as He suffered the wrath of God for sinners.

When life is hard as a follower of Jesus, think about Job's confidence in Job 19:25–27. Say the words aloud. Remember that they were true for Jesus as He faced the Cross. Take heart that they are true for you.

Day 19

Read Job 20

Many of us remember how the White Witch gives Edmund delicious Turkish delight to entice him to betray Aslan, in C. S. Lewis' famous book *The Lion, the Witch, and the Wardrobe*. It was sweet to his taste, but poisonous to his heart.

In the same way, Zophar now portrays evil as sweet in the mouth but deadly in its effects. In some ways, this next speech of Zophar (Job 20) is rather similar to Bildad's speech in chapter 18. Most of it consists of a vivid description of the punishment of God on the wicked. As with Bildad's speech, the similarities to Job's own experience are very strong; again, the implication is that Job must be a wicked man.

Zophar focuses first on how the enjoyment that wicked people get is short-lived. You need to understand, he says to Job, "that the mirth of the wicked is brief, the joy of the godless lasts but a moment" (Job 20:5). The wicked man may laugh, but he will not have the last laugh. He may enjoy successful pride, so that his "head touches the clouds" (v. 6); he may even become, Zophar might have implied, "the greatest man among all the people of the East" (1:3). But it won't be long before God brings him down (as He has done with Job), and he will simply disappear from this life (20:5–11).

Then, in verses 12–19, the focus moves to a picture of evil as something that tastes sweet but turns sour and proves poisonous (vv. 12–14). It may seem fun to oppress the poor and seize houses, but the fun won't last (vv. 19–22). Indeed, it will lead to God's burning anger, which the wicked man cannot escape (vv. 23–25).

How do these descriptions of hell speak to us today? First, they tell us, in very vivid and memorable terms, what hell will be like. Hell will be every bit as bad as Zophar, and Bildad in chapter 18, describe it. **We need to urgently proclaim the gospel to a world that is heading for hell.**

Second, they help us understand not only the pain of Job, but also something of what it cost the Lord Jesus to endure the wrath of God against sinners; for Jesus endured it though He did not deserve it, as Job had before Him.

Third, we are called in some way to share in the sufferings of Christ (Romans 8:17), and therefore the sufferings of Job. When we do, we will not be surprised.

ThinkThrough

Meditate on the depth of misery described in Job 20. Consider the reality of hell and pray for those you know who do not yet trust in Jesus.

Consider yourself and Christian brothers and sisters who are suffering today. See if you can discern points of similarity between their experience and those described by Zophar. Pray for them, and for yourself, if you are going through this. Take heart that Jesus went there first.

Day 20

Read Job 21

Do you live a good life? There used to be a television comedy called *The Good Life*. It was a play on the word "good", which can mean morally good (as opposed to evil) or enjoyable (as opposed to unpleasant).

Job's comforters are sure that these two always coincide. They believe that a man who lives a morally good life will enjoy a pleasant life, and that suffering is always evidence of moral wickedness. They deduce from Job's sufferings that Job must be wicked.

Job now takes them head-on. He demonstrates with powerful poetry that plenty of wicked people enjoy thoroughly pleasant lives. Lots of good things happen to bad people. "Why," he asks, "do the wicked live on, growing old and increasing in power?" (Job 21:7). He paints a picture of their happy families, their safe homes, their prosperous farms, their fun and parties, and their long lives of prosperity and peaceful deaths (vv. 7–13).

So, according to Job's comforters, they must be good people. Their blessings must be evidence of their moral goodness. But, says Job, not at all! Listen to their own words (vv. 14–15). They demonstrate by what they say that they care nothing for God. They just want God to leave them alone.

Of course, Job would admit that some wicked people get punished. But not many. In verses 17–21, he asks how often this happens. Mostly, these people escape calamity and live long, happy lives. Everybody dies, and whether they were wicked or good seems to make very little difference to whether they enjoyed their lives (vv. 22–26).

Job challenges his blind comforters to get out more, to ask "those who travel" (v. 29)—those who actually look at the world as it is—what they have found. They will discover that their system simply doesn't work. Even in their funerals, wicked people are honoured (vv. 32–33)!

Job concludes by rebuking his friends for their "nonsense" and "falsehood" (v. 34). **If good things happen to bad people, then is it not possible that bad things might happen to good people, which is indeed what has happened to Job?**

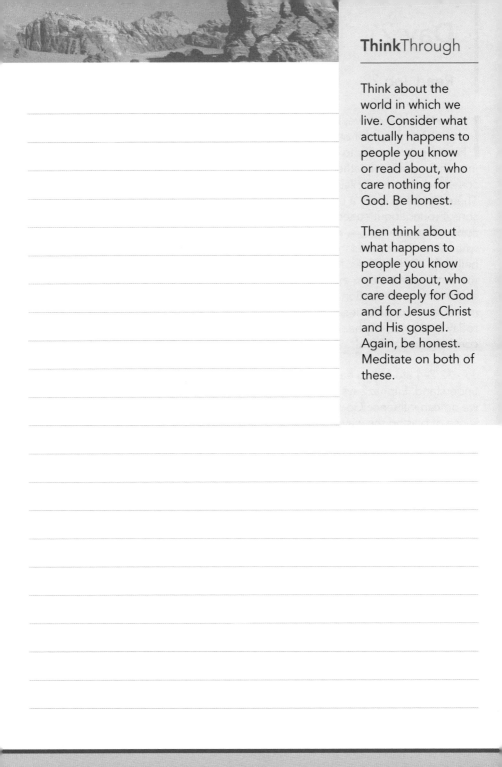

Think about the world in which we live. Consider what actually happens to people you know or read about, who care nothing for God. Be honest.

Then think about what happens to people you know or read about, who care deeply for God and for Jesus Christ and His gospel. Again, be honest. Meditate on both of these.

Read Job 22

I n the UK, where I live, most people are reluctant to confront somebody head-on. We prefer to hint or speak in roundabout ways rather than tell somebody that he is plain wrong. There has been quite a bit of this sort of roundabout speech between Job and his comforters. For example, when Bildad describes the terrors of hell (Job 18), he leaves Job to "join the dots" with his own experience and make the deduction that he, Job, must be an impenitent sinner. But in today's passage, Eliphaz is going to come right out with it!

Job 22:2–4 are not so easy to understand. Eliphaz says that nothing we do can influence God, in the sense of biasing the way He treats us. The idea is that God's treatment of us is 100 per cent consistent, and it depends entirely on our behaviour. There are no exceptions: good things happen consistently to good people, and bad things to bad people.

In verse 5, Eliphaz looks Job in the eye and says: "Is not your wickedness great? Are not your sins endless?" This is pretty strong! Job, you are far from blameless and upright—you are a terrible sinner! In verses 6–9, Eliphaz expands on Job's supposed sins: he has used his great power (v. 8), exploiting people who are weaker than himself, as so many powerful

men do. "*That is why* snares are all around you, why sudden peril terrifies you," he says (v. 10). Eliphaz has no evidence that would stand up in a court of law, but Job's terrible sufferings prove to him that Job *must* be a terrible sinner. How wrong he is!

In verses 12–20, Eliphaz, in line with what Bildad and Zophar have also said, insists that God can see Job's sins, however much he tries to hide them, and God will punish him for them. In his previous speech, Job had claimed that people who say to God, "Leave us alone!", often prosper (21:14)—but Eliphaz refutes this (22:20).

And so, in verses 21–30, Eliphaz closes his final speech with a beautiful and impassioned appeal to Job to repent. If Job would repent (the word "return" in verse 23 means "repent"), then God may restore and bless him. It is a beautiful and biblical appeal . . . so what is wrong with it? Everything! Job is not suffering because he is an impenitent sinner; we know from chapters 1 and 2 that Job is suffering precisely *because* he *is* blameless and upright. **These innocent sufferings reach their fulfilment in the cross of Christ and overflow today into the undeserved**

sufferings of the people of Christ who suffer with Him (Romans 8:17).

ThinkThrough

Do you expect a faithful Christian life to be accompanied by material and health blessings in this age? This is what prosperity preachers tell us. Think carefully about why it is simply not true.

When you suffer, ask yourself if you need a fresh repentance. But, if your conscience is clear, do not be surprised that you still suffer.

Day 22

Read Job 23

There is something frightening about invisibility. In fictional stories, when people can make themselves invisible, it gives them great power. You can't see where they are, where they are going, or what they are doing. Here, in this true story, God is invisible and Job is terrified.

And yet, even in his fear, Job longs to stand before the great invisible God. In today's reading and the next, we consider Job's reply to Eliphaz.

There are two sides to this reply. On the one hand (Job 23), Job longs for the day when he, and all others who are righteous by faith, will stand vindicated before God. On the other hand (Job 24), he yearns for the final judgment on the wicked. In a way, he prays, as we do in the Lord's Prayer, "Your will be done on earth as it is in heaven" (see Matthew 6:9–13).

In Job 23:1–7, Job says he longs to "find" the invisible God and state his case before Him. He believes that the day will come when he, along with all who are "upright" (that is, real believers; see 1:1, 8; 2:3), will be able to "establish their innocence before him" and "be delivered for ever" by God the judge (23:7). And yet, God is invisible (vv. 8–9): wherever Job looks, he cannot find Him!

Still, Job is sure that although he does not know the way God takes (as we saw in chapters 1 and 2, Job does not hear the heavenly scenes), God "knows the way that I take" (23:10).

God knows that Job walks with a clear conscience, that his "feet" (that is, his behaviour) closely follow God's ways, and that he has not departed from God's commands (vv. 11–12). So, Job is confident that "when he has tested me, I shall come forth as gold" (v. 10). Job knows that in this life, all manner of terrible things will happen to righteous and upright believers. **But he trusts that the day will come when God's will shall be done on earth as it is in heaven, and all true believers will be vindicated for ever.**

In verses 13–17, Job says how frightened he is of the great, all-powerful, invisible God. Yet he is confident, and his confidence is not a shallow thing. He is "not silenced" (v. 17), though there is awe and even terror in his heart as he contemplates final judgment.

When you think about the day of your death, does it thrill you to think you will stand before the Judge of all the earth? Be honest! Reflect on the sense of awe described in the hymn, *Rock of Ages, Cleft for Me*: "When I soar to worlds unknown, see Thee on Thy judgment throne . . ."

Have there been times in your life when you have longed deeply to see and know God, as Job does?

Day 23

Read Job 24

When a footballer commits a blatant foul and neither the referee nor the line judge blows the whistle, the other team's members will often gather round the referee gesticulating angrily. "Didn't you see that terrible thing that he did? Why don't you give him a red card, or at least give us a penalty?"

We are familiar with that sort of righteous indignation, the longing that a wrong should be put right. At a deeper level, this is what Job expresses in Job 24. His friends have repeatedly insisted that God *does* punish sinners; indeed, He punishes them without fail and quickly. This is why, they say, Job's sufferings are clear evidence that he must be such a sinner. But no, counters Job, it is not as simple as that.

Verse 1 asks the question which is the subject of this chapter: "Why does the Almighty not set times for judgment? Why must those who know him look in vain for such days?" God ought to come and judge, but He doesn't; why not? That is Job's question.

In verses 2–12, Job movingly describes both the crimes and—especially—the pain of the victims of those crimes. In verses 2–4, people shift boundary stones, steal sheep and valuable farm animals, and force poor people and widows into destitution. It is a scenario that is familiar in every economic context at every period of human history.

But look at the victims (vv. 5–8)! These poor people are forced to forage in wild places. Today, we see such people scavenging among rubbish piles around cities. The wicked have splendid vineyards (v. 6), but if you look carefully, you will see poor, desperate people scavenging there.

These victims are deprived of proper clothing and shelter (vv. 7–8). Why does God not act? People snatch children and traffic them as slaves (v. 9). Listen to the groans of these victims, wounded and dying by the unpunished wickedness of their powerful oppressors (vv. 10–12). Why does God not come to judge and bring justice? That is Job's question.

In verses 13–17, the catalogue of crimes continues with murder, theft, and adultery—and they all take place at night. These people turn day into night and night into day, reversing God's proper order of creation. Why does God not come to judge? That is Job's question.

It is not easy to understand the remainder of this chapter (vv. 18–25). **Probably, Job agrees with his friends that there will be a judgment. But he disagrees**

that judgment always comes now. No, he says, we have to wait. And, in the meantime, there is much injustice.

Take time to feel the pain and misery caused by human injustice in this world. Sometimes, we get so used to it that we become numb to the pain. Pray to feel how dreadful it is. Pray that God will send Jesus back and bring on the final judgment.

Think about the things we do that we think are unseen (Job 24:13–17). For example, an affair, pornography, tax evasion, or gossip on email. How would remembering that God sees everything influence your behaviour and actions?

Day 24

Read Job 25

Have you ever started speaking, then lapsed into an awkward silence when you ran out of things to say? It's embarrassing: you initially give the impression that you are persuasive and eloquent, but you end up stuttering and stammering.

Bildad is like that in today's reading. His third and final speech, in Job 25, is surprisingly short. It's rather pathetic, really. In a way, its brevity symbolises the bankruptcy of the tidy system of the comforters.

Bildad doesn't say much, but let's listen to what he does say. In verses 2 and 3, he begins to wax eloquent about the greatness and power of God. God has "dominion" and inspires "awe". He rules in the "heights of heaven", which speaks of His "place" of government of the universe—far above the ability of human beings to challenge Him. He has such huge armed forces that you can't count them. His power as Creator impacts everybody: there is no corner of the universe that can claim to be outside of God's power.

So far, so good: Job would agree, as would any believer.

But then, in verse 4, Bildad repeats what Eliphaz has said repeatedly (4:17; 15:14–16): because God is so awesomely great, it follows that no mortal human being can ever hope to be "righteous" (in the right) or "pure". That is to say, when Job arrogantly—as it seems to Bildad—wants to stand before God and be vindicated (23:1–7), he is chasing the moon. No mortal can hope for that, and it is outrageous and proud to think you can. After all, even the moon and the stars are not pure in God's eyes (25:5–6). No mortal can ever be more than "a maggot . . . a worm"!

And so, the speeches of these wise comforters, who bring the wisdom of the world to bear on Job and his sufferings, stutter to a halt. There is no gospel here. A God who is sovereign is true. Mortals who acknowledge our frail mortality are wise. But unless God provides a mediator who can enable Job to stand in the presence of God, there is no gospel. **Only when Job's undeserved sufferings are seen as the foreshadowing of the cross of Christ, can there be hope for mortal men and women.**

ThinkThrough

Ponder the greatness of God as Bildad describes it, for it is true. Bow before God in His majesty. But then, thank God that in Jesus we do have a Mediator who enables us to stand justified, pure, and righteous before this awesome God.

Think back over the speeches made by Job's comforters. What do they get right? And where do they go so terribly wrong?

Day 25

Read Job 26

Have you ever had to rebuke a friend with the use of biting sarcasm? To say something deeply cutting in order to try to get through to him? Something like: "Oh, you are *such* a kind friend to me. I really appreciate your thoughtful and gentle words"—when the reality is, he has been unkind and without understanding. Job has to do that in today's reading. This is his final speech in the three cycles of speeches.

Job begins with this biting sarcasm (Job 26:2–4), which I paraphrase: "I am so weak and feeble, and you have helped me so much! I had no wisdom, and you have really helped me to understand. I can't imagine the wonderful source you have for your wise and understanding words." (Or not!)

In verses 5–13, Job sings exultantly in praise of the sovereignty of God. This may surprise us, but one of the characteristics of Job's speeches is that he is inconsistent. His friends are consistent—their system is clear, but in their consistency, they are consistently wrong. Job, however, is inconsistent: sometimes, he struggles as he grapples with deep and painful things, though he grapples in faith; and, from time to time, his faith surfaces with a wonderful clarity.

In verses 5–6, Job praises God, saying that even when you go to the realm of the dead, the most remote, darkest, and wildest corner of the universe, even there, all is "naked before God". God sees it all, He knows it all, He rules it all. Even "Destruction" (referring to *Abaddon* in Hebrew, later *Apollyon* in Greek, the angel of the bottomless pit in Revelation 9:11) is under God's gaze and control.

Verses 7–10 poetically describe how God is sovereign over the whole world. And yet—and here Job goes beyond the tidy system of his friends—God has the power to make the creation order tremble in a kind of moral earthquake (v. 11). This is what is happening in Job's life, and it reaches its climax when the innocent Jesus dies and the earth shakes (Matthew 27:51).

The "Rahab" of Job 26:12 is the same as the "gliding serpent" of verse 13. This is the storybook monster who seeks to oppose the Creator. We shall meet it again under another name in chapter 41. In a way, this is Satan himself. And yet God is sovereign, even over supernatural evil. Nothing, absolutely nothing, is outside His control.

In 26:14, Job goes even further in his praise of God. He has sung the control of God over the whole universe, physical and spiritual. And yet this is "but the outer fringe of his works". **For there is more in the inscrutable wisdom of God than we can yet see.**

ThinkThrough

A church without the true gospel is empty and useless. Have you ever known supposed Christian teachers who deserve the sarcasm of Job 26:2–4?

Ponder on the awesome sovereignty of God. Set this against all the puzzles of Job's suffering, Jesus' suffering, and Christian suffering. Feel the awe as "the pillars of heaven quake" (Job 26:11), and bow before the inscrutable wisdom of God.

Day 26

Read Job 27

Have you ever watched a scene which turns out to be the opposite of what it appears to be? When Jesus the prisoner stands before Pontius Pilate the judge, it *looks* as if Jesus is in danger and Pilate has power. At one level, that is exactly what is happening: Pilate has the power to condemn Jesus to crucifixion. Yet, in a deeper reality, it is Jesus who will sit in judgment and Pilate who will stand condemned.

In a similar way, we see in Job 27 an ironic reversal of roles. Again and again, the "friends" of Job have described the judgment of God on the wicked in ways that echo the sufferings of Job. They leave Job to draw the conclusion that he must be a wicked man who needs to repent. Now, we shall listen as Job turns the tables.

The words, "Job continued his discourse" (Job 27:1), introduce each of Job's summing-up speeches (first in chapters 27–28, then in chapters 29–31). In chapter 27, he speaks to all three of his friends (notice the "you . . . all . . ." in verse 12).

Job begins by insisting that he is in the right with God (vv. 2–6). Even though God has—for a reason Job cannot understand—"denied" him "justice" (v. 2), he will not accept that his friends were right to accuse him of wickedness; rather, he will rather insist on his "integrity" and "innocence", for he has a clear "conscience" (vv. 5–6).

When Job's friends accuse him repeatedly of sins he has not committed, they make themselves his enemies. And because they set themselves against Job, they make themselves enemies of God. This is the logic of verses 7–10. **Any adversary of Job is an enemy of God, because Job belongs to God.** In a similar way, centuries later, just as it was dangerous to oppose Jesus (whom Job foreshadows), so it is dangerous to harm the people of Jesus, because they, too, belong to God.

In verses 11–23, Job describes "the fate God allots to the wicked" (v. 13). It is a terrifying description, not unlike the pictures his friends have painted (for example, by Bildad in 18:5–21). But the tables are turned here. Job's friends described the wicked because they wanted to show that *he* was wicked. Here, Job describes the wicked because *they* are being wicked when they oppose him; they are therefore in great danger.

Think about how hard it is to suffer for Jesus. Consider the persecuted church or friends who are being attacked because they are Christians. Now, consider the even greater danger that those who do the persecuting are in. Pray for these poor endangered souls in the miserable plight of their hostility to God.

Examine your conscience. Can you, like Job, insist that you really are in a right relation-ship with God (Job 26:2–6) even when everything is going wrong in your life? Seek the joyful assurance of a clear and cleansed conscience.

Day 27

Read Job 28

Have you ever wondered how your phone or tablet works? When something goes wrong with it, you long for an expert to come alongside you and tell you what's going on. You want to know its architecture, how it is structured inside. On a grander scale, we also want to know the underlying architecture of the universe. By what rules does the world operate? We can see what happens, but why does it happen? We long to know why, especially when we suffer.

In Job 28, Job gives us a most wonderful and thought-provoking poem. Verses 1–11 are about mining. As we read through the poem, we are invited to think about two things. First, is what we are mining for as valuable as silver, gold, iron, copper, and precious stones? Mining is worth doing because the rewards are so valuable (vv. 6, 10).

The second theme is about how difficult these rewards are to get. Mining is hard and costly; miners—especially in those early days—risked their lives in darkness, far away from where people lived, going to a place that even the sharp-eyed birds of prey could not see (vv. 3–4, 7–8).

But why did Job write this poem? Answer: because he wants to talk about something even more valuable than gold and jewels—wisdom, for which a search is even more difficult. These are the themes of verses 12–22.

Wisdom here means the architecture or blueprint of the universe. It includes what we call scientific laws, like gravity, as well as the moral laws of the world—how good deeds are related to blessing, and bad deeds to suffering. Where can the answer to these deep puzzles be found? This is the question of verses 12 and 20. And the answer is: we can't hope to find it.

But God knows the answers (vv. 23–27). He doesn't tell us, but He knows. Our task is to fear Him with reverent, believing fear and to shun evil (v. 28) —in other words, to do just what Job has been doing all along (1:1,8; 2:3)! **We cannot expect to know the answers, but we are to walk in loving fellowship with God, who does know the answers.**

This is what Job does; it will be what Jesus does on earth; and it is what we are to do. As you face the challenges of each new day, take time not just to puzzle over what is going on in your life, but also to ask yourself what it would mean to fear God with loving, reverent fear, and to turn away from evil.

Meditate on the mining poem in Job 28. Now, think about wisdom: How does the poem make you really want it, and yet know that you can't have it (in this ultimate sense)?

Now, meditate on Job 28:28. Resolve to be one who truly loves and fears God and repents daily of evil. Then, trust God for the outcome.

Day 28

Read Job 29

Picture the scene. A great leader, a president or a prime minister, enters the council chamber of government. Everybody stands. Nobody speaks. Half-finished sentences die out. All eyes are on this great leader as he takes his seat. Why? Is it because they are frightened of him, as they might be of a dictator? It might be.

But there is another possibility. Sometimes, respect is genuine. It comes because a ruler deserves it. I remember watching the funeral of former British prime minister Winston Churchill when I was a young boy. I was moved as the great cranes in the London docklands dipped their heads before the memorial flypast. Despite his faults, he was a great man. We, the people of Britain, knew we owed our freedom to his courage.

Job was such a great man. And in his greatness, he anticipates a greater man.

Job 29-31 is Job's second and final summing-up speech. The words, "Job continued his discourse", introduce this speech, as they did the previous one (chapters 27–28). The speech is divided into three clear parts, corresponding to chapters 29, 30, and 31. In chapter 29, Job reflects on life before the disasters of chapters 1–2. There are at least two surprises about what he valued most in those days.

First, in verses 2–6, what he had treasured and what he now misses is not so much the blessings (the health and the wealth), but the joy of fellowship with God. Job remembers when "God watched over me" (v. 2), "when God's intimate friendship blessed my house" (v. 4), and "when the Almighty was still with me" (v. 5). More than the blessings, it is God he loves.

The second surprise comes in verses 7–25. When Job describes his blessings, his focus is not on his wealth or pleasures. It is on his greatness as a leader who brought blessings to his people. He was treated with great respect (vv. 7–10) because he "rescued the poor" (v. 12), looked after the needy (vv. 12–16), punished the oppressor (v. 17), and comforted the mourner (v. 25). **In his greatness, Job anticipates a greater King who will walk in fellowship with the Father and bring blessings to His people.**

Job naturally expected to live a long and pain-free life (vv. 18–20). But it is not to be. And one of the main points of the book of Job is to understand why this great and righteous man must suffer.

Meditate on Job's love for God. Then consider how deeply Jesus loved the Father and treasured His intimate friendship with Him. Now, ask God to give you that same love, so that you value not your health or wealth, but your intimate friendship with God.

Think about how Jesus more than fulfilled the greatness of Job as described in Job 29:7–25. Thank God for Him and pray to be like Him in the small areas of life where you can have an influence to help the needy.

Day 29

Read Job 30

Our *Mutual Friend* is the last novel completed by Charles Dickens. It contains some particularly evil rogues. Mr Riderhood is perhaps the worst. There is nothing redeeming about this dreadful blackmailer, murderer, and deceiver. He is utterly terrible.

In this next part of Job's summing-up speech, we will see him being treated worse than a man such as Mr Riderhood deserves. A man who was, and deserves to be, the highest of the high, will descend so low that he becomes the lowest of the low.

Job 29 had looked back to a glorious past. Chapter 30 is trapped in a miserable present; notice the refrain: "But now . . . And now . . . And now . . ." (vv. 1, 9, 16). Verses 1–8 describe the people who now laugh at Job and mock him. They are "younger" (v. 1) than Job in a culture that rightly honours seniority. The focus in verses 2–8 is not so much on their poverty as on their moral worthlessness. These are not the virtuous poor; these are good-for-nothings, unemployable, "base" people (v. 8), the kind who are rightly kept far from society. And yet, Job is treated as lower even than them!

In verses 9–15, we hear these people singing rude songs about Job, spitting at him, kicking him, and terrifying him. And all because, as they judge, "God

has . . . afflicted me" (v. 11). Job is treated as a God-forsaken man.

Poor Job will cry out to God in desperate prayer (vv. 20–23), but God will not answer him. He cries for help (v. 24), he weeps for others, but his weeping for himself is not heard.

In some strange way, it is necessary that this great and good man should suffer as he does. We who have read the heavenly scenes in chapters 1 and 2 know that **Job's suffering is necessary to demonstrate the genuineness of his faith**. But Job does not know this, and may never know it until after his death. To him, it is bewildering. The descriptions of his sufferings are achingly sad. He is so lonely, and has become the companion of jackals and owls howling and crying in the night (v. 29), but nobody hears him.

And so we see God's good order of creation turned inside out and upside down. We know that these sufferings foreshadow the terrors of the cross of Christ, and that they share the character of Christ's redemptive suffering. But, for Job, it is a prison of present-tense misery, and he laments with great depth and pathos.

Meditate on those who mocked Job and those who mocked Jesus on the cross. Consider how their mockery demonstrates their unworthiness. Ponder the strange reason why it is necessary that one so great and so good—first Job, then Jesus—should be brought so very low.

Remember that followers of Jesus are asked to take up the cross and walk in His footsteps (Luke 9:23). Pray that you would be willing to walk this way even when it is desperately painful.

Read Job 31

When a soccer player dives and the referee penalises him with a red card, he will often protest his innocence. He will wave his hands as if to say, "What?! How outrageous to think I would cheat!"

We are used to being sceptical about such claims of innocence. When people say, "I'm in the right; I don't deserve this," we are naturally dubious. We have seen too many examples of guilty people claiming to be innocent.

But Job is an exception. In this last part of his final speech in Job 31, we hear him repeatedly claiming innocence. When we reread Job 1:1, 8 and 2:3, and look ahead to Job 42:7, we must remember that Job is indeed a righteous and blameless believer. **He is not sinless, and does not claim to be. But he is a forgiven sinner walking through life before God with a clear conscience.**

Job begins by speaking of "a covenant with (his) eyes not to look lustfully at a young woman" (31:1). But it probably stands for all wrong desires. Job agrees that wrong desires deserve to be punished. But he is walking before God "in the light", as John will later put it (1 John 1:7).

In Job 31:4–6, Job challenges God to weigh him, to vindicate him as "blameless". And then, in verses 7–34, he offers a catalogue of the kinds of sins he might have committed, but hasn't. This list doesn't include every possible sin, but it contains quite a few. In each case, Job says something like this: if I had committed this sin, then God would be right to punish me, because it would be wrong. But, in fact, I have not. Job repeatedly claims to be a righteous and innocent man.

The list includes dishonesty (vv. 7–8), adultery (vv. 9–12), treating junior people unfairly (vv. 13–15), not being generous to people in need (vv. 16–20), using his power against the fatherless (that is, the defenceless) (vv. 21–23), trusting in his wealth (vv. 24–25), worshipping created things (vv. 26–28), being pleased when bad things happen to his enemies (vv. 29–30), not being hospitable to travellers (vv. 31–32), and being a hypocrite (vv. 33–34).

In verses 35–37, Job boldly challenges God himself to consider his case. It is as though his final defence statement has been typed up, and he now signs it. And, by signing it, he challenges God to vindicate him. It is an extraordinarily

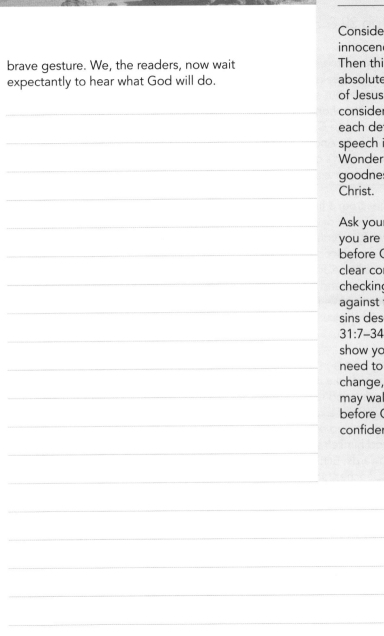

brave gesture. We, the readers, now wait expectantly to hear what God will do.

ThinkThrough

Consider the innocence of Job. Then think about the absolute sinlessness of Jesus when considered against each detail of this speech in Job 31. Wonder at the sheer goodness of Jesus Christ.

Ask yourself if you are walking before God with a clear conscience, checking yourself against the list of sins described in Job 31:7–34. Ask God to show you where you need to repent and change, that you too may walk in the light before God with confident assurance.

Day 31

Read Job 32 & 33

God whispers to us in our pleasures, speaks in our conscience, but shouts in our pains: it is His megaphone to rouse a deaf world. So wrote C. S. Lewis in *The Problem of Pain*. And it is true. Suffering may be God's mercy to us, to bring us to our senses.

The idea comes from a little-known character in the book of Job. At the start of chapter 32, a young man called Elihu is introduced (vv. 1–5). Elihu is angry because Job is accusing God of being unjust and because Job's three friends have failed to persuade him otherwise. So, Elihu begins to answer Job.

Although many commentators think Elihu is ambiguous, like Job's three friends, there are good reasons for thinking he is actually a reliable and prophetic voice, a kind of "warm up" before God himself speaks from chapter 38 onwards. Elihu makes four unanswered speeches. Job 32–33 is the first.

In chapter 32:6–22, Elihu explains why he has decided to speak, despite being younger than the others. He is dismayed that God has been accused of injustice and no one has answered this accusation. So, he begins. In chapter 33, he gives the first part of his answer. First, he reassures Job that he need not be terrified of him

(vv. 1–7). Then, he summarises what Job has been saying (vv. 8–11). Next, he contradicts Job's claim that God has refused to speak to him (vv. 12–13). "For," says Elihu, "God does speak" (v. 14). The question is: How? Elihu gives two answers.

First, God speaks through what seems to be conscience, as a man with a guilty conscience has a frightening dream (vv. 15–18).

Second, God speaks through pain (vv. 19–28). As someone draws "near to the pit" (that is, death, v. 22), God sends some kind of messenger to be gracious to him, to provide a ransom for him, to restore him to health, and to bring him back to God (vv. 23–25). It is not an easy passage to understand in detail, but the idea seems to be this: God uses pain to bring us back to Him. In the same way, God is speaking to Job to call him to himself. Elihu concludes by urging Job to listen to his message (vv. 29–33).

Elihu is right and what he says is profound. **God does indeed speak to us through our guilty consciences, and He does use suffering to bring us to Him in faith.** Even though Job is not an impenitent sinner, this message should be a comfort to him.

Think about the times when God worked in your life through your conscience, perhaps when God roused your conscience and you were troubled in the night. Thank God for His mercy.

Then, consider the times in your life, or in the life of another Christian, when God used suffering, pain, or disappointment to draw you or them closer to Him. Thank Him for this kindness too.

Read Job 34

When an astronaut sits strapped into his small cabin on top of a rocket, he knows that his safety depends on the integrity of those who have made the rocket. If they made it well, he should succeed and live; but if they cut corners and made careless mistakes, the rocket will disintegrate and he will die.

In a slightly similar way, the survival of the cosmos depends on the justice and faithfulness of the God who made it. If the Creator God were unjust, then the whole universe would disintegrate. This is at the heart of Elihu's second speech.

In Job 34:1–15, Elihu speaks to a wider audience (using plural verbs). Let us think about "what is right . . . what is good", he says (v. 4). Job accuses God of mistreating him (vv. 5–6) and this is outrageous (vv. 7–9). For, insists Elihu, God will never "do evil . . . do wrong" but is always just and fair (vv. 10–11). "It is unthinkable that God would do wrong" (v. 12) because He governs the whole world and we would all perish without a trace if God were not just (vv. 13–15).

Then, from verse 16 to the end of the chapter, Elihu speaks to Job personally (using singular verbs). He rebukes Job for suggesting that the one who governs the world can do wrong (vv. 16–17). On the contrary (vv. 18–30), God shows no favouritism (v. 19), knows perfectly what is happening (vv. 21–24), and punishes people for their wickedness (vv. 25–30).

Job has denied these axiomatic truths and must repent of these wrong things he has said. And Elihu is right: Job has indeed said some wrong things about God. At the end of God's speeches, he will repent of what he has said (see 40:1–5; 42:1–6). Elihu makes a very profound point which is precisely right. **Because God is the Creator, He must —He simply must—act with righteousness.** The idea that God could actually bend the rules of justice would endanger the fabric of the cosmos.

At the end of the book, we realise a paradox: Job is a real and blameless believer (1:1,8; 2:3), yet he has also said some things he ought not to have said, and of which he will need to repent. Elihu is a voice that will begin to prepare Job to repent. He will need to hear the greater voice of God; but Elihu has a preparatory role here.

"It is unthinkable that God would do wrong" (Job 34:12). Meditate on this. Consider deeply how much it matters that this is precisely true.

Think of the times when you might have accused God of acting wrongly or unfairly. Repent, even when you cannot yet understand how God can be right in what He is doing.

Day 33

Read Job 35

D on't say that; you will make God sad. Poor God feels hurt by what you say. We easily slip into saying things like that. But they are quite wrong, as we shall see!

In this third speech, Elihu attacks something Job has been saying or implying: "What profit is it to me, and what do I gain by not sinning?" (Job 35:3). Job has begun to ask the prosperity gospel question: If I am pious and it doesn't do me any good, what's the point of being pious? Elihu answers this robustly in two ways.

First, in verses 5–8, he invites Job to look up at the sky, which is a picture of the greatness of God. God is far above this world, so very high. He is so far above us that, on the one hand, if we sin, we don't affect God, we don't "do" anything to God (v. 6); we can't hurt God or damage Him with our sins. On the other hand, even if we are righteous, we don't give anything to God, we don't benefit God, we can't put God in our debt (v. 7). The technical words are that God is transcendent (far above us), impassible (He cannot suffer), and immutable (He is unchangeable).

Elihu is right. God is all these things. It is therefore a great mistake to think that we can affect God by what we do, and therefore expect God to respond by blessing or cursing us.

The blessing and cursing of God is a deeper matter than simple cause and effect.

Second, in verses 9–16, Elihu takes the argument a step further. In verses 9–13, he observes that all over the world, people suffering oppression cry out in some sense towards God (v. 9). However—and this is the point—they don't usually ask, "Where is God my Maker?" (v. 10). That is, they don't genuinely seek God in their hearts. They cry out, but they do not truly pray. And that is why God doesn't answer this kind of cry; their plea is "empty" (vv. 12–13). In verses 14–16, Elihu applies this to Job. The reason God has not as yet answered him is that his talk is "empty" too (v. 16).

It would seem that Job has begun to slip into the mistaken logic of the prosperity gospel, expecting God to hear him, answer him, and bless him, *because* of his piety. Elihu rightly rebukes him for this kind of slot-machine view of God.

Ask yourself if you have slipped into thinking that God is like us and can be made happier or sadder by what we do. Repent and seek a truer and greater view of the almighty grandeur of the God who is far above us.

Do you ever slip into thinking that God owes you blessing because you have been obedient, trusting, or virtuous? Repent of this and bow before Him simply because He is God (as Job had done at the start).

Read Job 36 & 37

To govern the universe, you need to understand everything and control everything. God does both. This is the main thrust of Elihu's final and grandest speech. His purpose is to "ascribe justice to my Maker" (Job 36:2–4), to demonstrate to Job that the God he worships is both great and good, both all-powerful and all-wise.

First, Elihu speaks about how God governs people in the world (vv. 5–25). He does punish evildoers (v. 6), and He will restore the righteous (that is, those who are righteous by faith) (vv. 6–7). Sometimes—perhaps not infrequently—people who trust God are "held fast by cords of affliction" (v. 8), but this is God's kind discipline, intended to save them in the end (vv. 9–10), if they will "listen to correction". Some will respond well (v. 11), but others will not (vv. 12–14). In verses 16–25, Elihu appeals to Job: God "is wooing you from the jaws of distress" (v. 16), so you must be careful not to say about God what you ought not to say, for God is very great.

Then, from 36:26 to the end of chapter 37, Elihu speaks with great power about God's government of the whole world. "How great is God," he begins, "beyond our understanding!" (36:26). God is beyond and outside of time (v. 26). Things like the process of water evaporation, formation of clouds, and rainfall are beyond our understanding, but are clearly meant for our good (vv. 27–28), as are the terrifying processes of thunderstorms (vv. 29–33). Elihu is filled with awe at the majesty of the God who directs and controls the great storms of the world, and the storms of life (37:1–13).

From 37:14, Elihu appeals directly to Job: "Listen to this, Job; stop and consider God's wonders." Think about the power of God seen in the storm, and consider the infinite wisdom of the God who directs these wild phenomena, so that every bolt of lightning and every clap of thunder is under His direction and control.

From verse 21, the storm is over, and Elihu meditates on the beauty of the light after the storm, on the "awesome majesty" (v. 22) of the God who directs the storm, and on the (same) God who brings beauty after the storm. **The proper response to this great God is to "revere him" (v. 24), to bow before Him, and never to think that we know better than God on how to govern His world.**

With his emphasis on the power and the wisdom of God, Elihu is a sort of an Elijah figure who prepares the way for the Lord himself to speak.

ThinkThrough

Read aloud the description of the storm (Job 36:26–37:24). Allow the feelings of awe to move you to adoration and humble worship before the God of the storm, the sovereign, all-wise Creator.

Repent of the times when you have begun to think you could govern the world better than God.

Day 35

Read Job 38:1–21

Have you ever stood, or tried to stand, in the midst of hurricane winds? Hurricanes are rare in the UK, where I live, but I did once walk on a hilltop amid what I later discovered had been hurricane-force winds. It was frightening.

In the book of Job, a huge storm is a picture of the power of God and of the troubles enveloping Job. The storm so vividly described by Elihu in Job 37 is the context for the covenant God himself to speak. Yes, now, finally, God speaks individually to Job (38:1)!

The speech in today's reading is a rebuke, for Job has spoken "words without knowledge" (vv. 2–3). He is not guilty of secret sins, as his friends say, but he has said wrong things about God. God asks a series of questions, and the answer to each one is: "No, I haven't; but I admit that You have."

There are five sections in today's passage. The big theme is how evil fits into creation.

In verses 4–7, the universe is described as a building with foundations. When God finished it, there was a great song of joy, for the universe was (and still is) very good! C. S. Lewis picked up this imagery in *The Magician's Nephew*, when Aslan sings Narnia into existence.

In verses 8–11, we meet "the sea". In Bible imagery, the sea stands for chaos and disorder which threatens the stable, dry land on which we can live. Here, the sea, like a badly-behaved child, has limits fixed for it. God has placed limits on evil, as He did when Satan asked to attack Job in chapters 1 and 2.

Verses 12–15 teach us that evil will not last. Every time the sun rises and the darkness of the night is dispelled, it reminds us that one day, all wickedness will disappear.

Verses 16–18 are about the place of the dead, which is at the bottom of the sea in Bible imagery. This is the most extreme place in creation. And yet, even here God sees and knows.

Verses 19–21 look at some more extremes—the end of the east, where the sun rises, and the end of the west, where it sets. However far you go in the universe, God sees, God knows, God controls.

Evil has a strange place in God's universe for the moment. But it is all under His control, and it will not last.

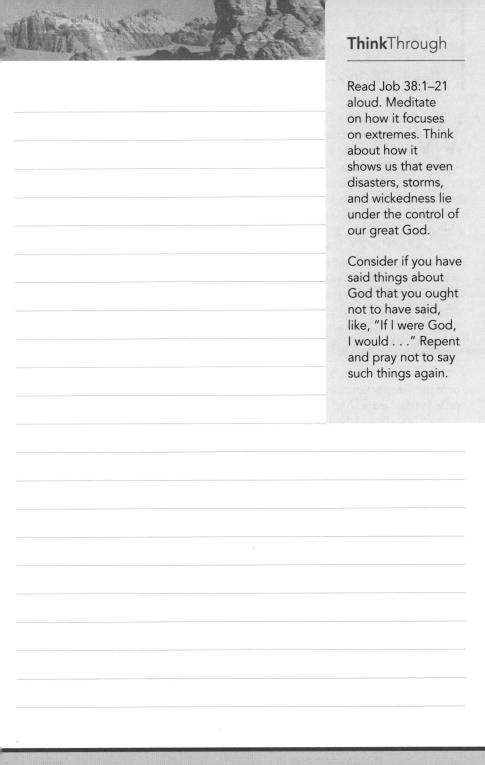

ThinkThrough

Read Job 38:1–21 aloud. Meditate on how it focuses on extremes. Think about how it shows us that even disasters, storms, and wickedness lie under the control of our great God.

Consider if you have said things about God that you ought not to have said, like, "If I were God, I would . . ." Repent and pray not to say such things again.

Day 36

Read Job 38:22–38

Water is such a fascinating substance. Have you ever thought about what water can do? Perhaps you have struggled in a big hailstorm and have experienced the destructive force of water. Or, you have coped with a bitterly cold winter, and snow has been your challenge. Maybe a huge rainstorm accompanied by strong winds has threatened your home. Or, perhaps you have enjoyed the soft dew on the grass in the morning or been glad for the rain showers that make your garden grow.

In this next part of God's first speech, there are five sections. In four of them, water is the theme. And yet, still the theme of evil lies in the background to what God says.

Job 38:22–24 conjure up pictures of violent winter storms, of war and trouble. Heavy rain falls, and frozen hail, dangerous snow, thunderstorms, and lightning are highlighted. It is all very frightening, and it paints a picture of so much of Job's current life situation. And yet, it is all under God's control.

Verses 25–27 talk about water bringing life. Even though it may begin with a storm (v. 25), the result is water flowing to remote areas far from human irrigation. And so, things grow. The same water is used by God for destruction and for life.

Verses 28–30 form a lovely quiet poem about how water and God are related. God is the "father" and the "womb" from which water comes; He is intimately related to His creation. Some of this water comes from God as dew, to bring life, and some of it as ice and frost, to make life hard. Somehow, God the Creator is behind each and all of these.

In verses 31–33, we leave water to look at the stars. The Pleiades, Orion, and the Bear are constellations of stars. People thought—and still think (with horoscopes)—that the stars control affairs on earth. That isn't true. No! God is sovereign and controls the stars.

Then in verses 34–38, we come back to water. God is the commander giving orders to the clouds and the lightning bolts, telling them where, when, and how to fall.

Through our tour of the different states and uses of water, we see a vivid picture of how the one good Creator controls and directs all things—including things that seem chaotic or dangerous to us—as He wishes. We can trust Him.

Think about the most extreme weather you have known or seen in videos. Consider how destructive it can be. Then, meditate that even this comes from the "womb" of God. Bow in worship and trust Him.

Now think about life-giving rainfall and thank God for the blessings of rain as a sign of all His blessings that make life possible.

Day 37

Read Job 38:39–40:5

We live in a world in which violence is thought to be always wrong. But, is it? Picture two scenes in a nature film. First, we see hungry lion cubs crying for food. Then, we see them eating happily. What has happened in between? Answer: the lion or lioness has hunted prey and killed it violently! So, is this evil or good? We need to think carefully about this, and the next section of God's speech prompts us to do that.

The focus shifts to animals and birds, especially the wild ones. There is a particular emphasis on life and death in the wild.

First, Job 38:39–41 take us to that scene of lions and lion cubs, and also the raven, who feeds on the carcasses killed by predators like lions. When God asks Job, "Do you hunt the prey?" (v. 39), He is implying that while Job doesn't, He—God—does! The whole food chain is under God's command.

Then, in 39:1–4, the camera takes us out into the mountains as we watch remote mountain goats getting pregnant, going into labour, giving birth, and then their young growing and leading their own lives. Who is behind the remote saga of new life? God is.

From the wild goat, 39:5–8 take us to the wild donkey. Far from the farm, this creature roams free. And yet, even here, far from human dwelling, God provides the food it needs.

In 39:9–12, we meet the wild ox, a very large horned creature. With some humour, Job is asked if he can tame it, and of course, he can't! For this creature is wild and untameable. And yet, in all its wild power, it is under the control of God.

There is a very funny little cameo in 39:13–18, the ostrich! She is silly (for she doesn't care very well for her young) and extremely fast. She is just odd. And yet, in her oddness, she is not outside the knowledge or power of God.

39:19–25 paint a terrifying and magnificent portrait of the war horse, the nuclear weapon of the ancient world. This most powerful of creatures is also under the power of God.

Finally, in 39:26–30, we come back to the food chain. Here, the birds of prey, the hawk or the eagle, are in view. They live high up, in very remote places. And they hunt prey for their young.

Then, in 40:1–2, God rebukes Job for arguing with Him, for thinking he can run the world better than God can. Job admits that he is not as important as he thought, and says he will stop talking (vv. 3-5).

Imagine all these wild creatures as you read Job 38:39–40:5 aloud. As you do, think about your own insignificance and weakness, and meditate on the Creator's infinite wisdom and strength.

As in the last reading, repent afresh for times or ways in which you have thought you could run God's world better than He does.

Day 38

Read Job 40:6–24

In the movie *Bruce Almighty*, TV reporter Bruce Nolan complains once too often about how God is running the world. So, God puts Nolan in charge for a while to see how he will cope. It's a silly movie, and possibly rather blasphemous. But the main point is to laugh at the complete mess that this complaining reporter gets into when he tries to run the world.

In the LORD's second speech (Job 40:6–41:34), God again asks Job to "brace yourself like a man, I will question you, and you shall answer me" (40:7; see 38:3). He rebukes Job for discrediting His justice and condemning Him (vv. 6–8). Job still has not learned what he needs to learn. The second speech is more than a postscript to the first. For in this second speech, God says something much greater than He does in the first.

In verses 9–14, God gives Job an imaginary challenge. Why don't you put on My royal robes, Job? Go on, "adorn yourself with glory and splendour, and clothe yourself in honour and majesty" (v. 10). Then, when you have put on My royal and judicial clothes, set about being angry with proud, wicked people (vv. 11–12). And don't just be angry with them; bring them down to the "dust"—that is, end their lives (v. 13). Bring them right down to the place of the dead.

And then, when you have dealt with all the wicked, "I myself will admit to you that your own right hand can save you" (v. 14). Go on, have a go! But of course, **wickedness is much too strong and perplexing for Job to deal with on his own. Only the judge of all the earth (Genesis 18:25) can do this.**

After this, there is a portrait of a magnificent and frightening land creature called "Behemoth" (Job 40:15–24). Some have thought this to be a hippopotamus, for there are some similarities. Behemoth is very strong, lives by the river, and eats grass. But it would seem that Behemoth (which means something like "super beast") refers to something supernatural or extinct, something more frightening than you could ever find in a zoo today. Perhaps he is Death personified, a far cry from the persona of death we sometimes see drawn in cartoons— a hooded figure with a sickle.

Job not only cannot defeat this beast, but he doesn't understand how this victory will be achieved. For it will only be by the death of Jesus Christ in the place of sinners, that the devil and death itself will be defeated (Hebrews 2:14). And yet, even though Job does not understand this, by a strange paradox, his innocent sufferings foreshadow that great and future victory.

ThinkThrough

Have you ever wondered if you could govern the world better than God? Perhaps, you see innocent suffering and can't understand why God allows it. Meditate on the challenge of Job 40:6–24 and repent. Remember that God alone has the wisdom and power to defeat evil.

Look ahead from Job to the cross of Christ. Take a moment to thank Jesus for dying on the cross to defeat death and Satan!

Day 39

Read Job 41:1–42:6

Have you read *The Hound of the Baskervilles* by Arthur Conan Doyle? It is one of the best-known of the Sherlock Holmes stories. It features a terrifying hound, "an enormous coal-black hound, but not such a hound as mortal eyes have ever seen." The fear felt in the story is a small echo of the terror we are supposed to feel when we read the description of Leviathan in Job 41.

Finally, in the climax of God's second speech, He challenges Job to tame Leviathan. The description of this monster is supposed to terrify us. Imagine some vast sea monster, a many-headed sea serpent, with astonishing power and devastating ferocity. Then, multiply what you imagine by ten. This is the picture painted in chapter 41.

The Bible speaks of Leviathan elsewhere. Back in Job 3:8, we saw that he is a creature who has the power to delete Job's conception day or birthday from the calendar! In Isaiah 27:1, again he is a terrifying sea monster. In Psalm 74:12–14, he is a many-headed sea serpent; and when God defeats him, He establishes His power over day and night, sun and moon. Elsewhere, beasts are pictures of supernatural evil; we meet this imagery in the books of Daniel and Revelation (e.g., Daniel 7; Revelation 12:9, 20:2).

The monster Leviathan is a vivid picture to help us understand Satan. In his terribleness, it conveys to us something of the dark supernatural power of Satan and all his leagues of fallen angels. Here is a beast with the power of death.

Besides conjuring up the terror of Satan, the poem in Job 41 teaches us two things. First, and most obviously, Job is no match for this power. To be the judge of all the earth, Job will have to exercise power over Satan and all the hidden powers of evil in the universe. He cannot do this.

Second, and most strikingly, Leviathan or Satan is a creature and has no power independent of God. Verse 10 is important: if Leviathan is fierce (and he is), "Who then is able to stand against me" (v. 10)—that is, God? God controls Satan; Satan is, as Martin Luther vividly put it, "God's Satan". God is good; Satan is evil. But Satan has no independence from God. **In some strange and wonderful way, the good and all-powerful God governs and directs even the powers of evil in the universe!**

Job responds by admitting that God "can do all things", that He really does have complete and sovereign

power over the whole universe, evil included (42:2). And now, at last, he repents with deep humility (v. 6).

Read Job 41 aloud and feel the terrifying power of supernatural evil. How have you experienced the dark power of evil in your own life or the lives of those you love?

Praise God that He is sovereign even over the darkest of such dark powers. Admit to God again that He really can do all things and no purpose of His can be thwarted.

Day 40

Read Job 42:7–17

All's well that ends well, we say. And the story of Job does end well. Very well! But we need to be careful how we read it and apply it to ourselves.

The prose conclusion of the book begins with a rebuke (Job 42:7). Eliphaz reappears to represent himself, Bildad, and Zophar. In verse 7, God rebukes them for not speaking the truth about Him. Their message denied undeserved suffering, and therefore (in anticipation) denied the possibility of the cross of Christ. It therefore undermined the gospel. By contrast, Job, for all his mistakes, has fundamentally spoken with the voice of a believer.

So, no doubt to Eliphaz's great surprise, Job is the righteous man who needs to intercede for his friends! Acting as priest, he offers a sacrifice for them, and as intercessor, he prays for them and they are forgiven (vv. 8–9). Job here foreshadows the Lord Jesus, our great High Priest and Intercessor, by whose sacrifice and intercession His people are forgiven.

And then, we have a wonderful catalogue of blessings, far more abundant than even what Job had enjoyed at the start of the story (vv. 10–15). Grace is poured out upon him and the story ends with fullness of joy, love, beauty, and goodness.

It is important for us to understand this in the context of the whole Bible. James 5:7–11 encourages believers to "be patient . . . until the Lord's coming" (v. 7)—that is, until Jesus returns. To help them, James gives the example of "Job's perseverance" under trial (v. 11). Job persevered to the end of his story and then received blessing. We are to persevere until Jesus returns, on which we, too, will receive the blessings given to us in the new heaven and new earth.

When we read it in the context of the whole Bible, the book of Job does not teach what the prosperity gospel teaches, that is, that we may expect these blessings now. God may and does give us many blessings now, but the great blessings foreshadowed here are for when Jesus returns. **In the overall Bible story, Christian believers are still in the middle of the book of Job, learning to persevere under trial and to keep trusting, confident that the blessings will come to us at the end.**

ThinkThrough

Meditate on the wonder that Jesus, whose sufferings Job foreshadows, has offered a sacrifice for us and intercedes for us. May we, like Job, repent of saying wrong things about God, and may we take comfort from the intercession of Jesus.

Think about the wonderful blessings that Job received at the end. Look forward to love, beauty, joy, and plenty on the day when Jesus returns. Pray for grace to keep on trusting under trial.

Going Deeper
in Your Walk
with Christ

Whether you're a new Christian or have been a Christian for a while, it's worth taking a journey through the Bible, book by book, to gain a deeper appreciation of who Jesus is and how we can follow Him.

Let faithful Bible teachers be your tour guides and help you draw closer to Christ as you spend time reading and reflecting on His Word.

Journey Through

Amos

The book of Amos contains some hard messages that their original listeners would have found difficult to swallow. Yet, amid the unrelenting warnings of judgment, we can find assurances of God's love and compassion. Journey through Amos, and discover how the strident call to repentance comes with the comforting promise of restoration.

J.R. Hudberg and his wife, Heidi, live in Grand Rapids, Michigan, with their two young boys. He was born in Grand Rapids and attended college in Canada (where he met Heidi). After spending time in Ohio, Montana, and California, he returned "home". In the garden, on a boat, or in the woods, J.R. spends as much time as he can with family and friends enjoying God's creation. He is the executive editor for Our Daily Bread Ministries' *Discovery Series* booklets and is a regular contributor to the Insights for *Our Daily Bread*.

Journey Through
Hosea

by David Gibb

As God's spokesman, Hosea is told by Him to marry Gomer, a prostitute, and to go again and again to woo her back despite her many infidelities. Hosea's commitment to love Gomer gives us a glimpse of God's love for us. God loves His people as passionately and as jealously as a devoted husband loves his wife. Even when we wander from Him and our hearts cool towards Him, He continues to come after us and to draw us back to Him. God's love will never let us go. Rekindle your love and commitment to the One who loves you!

David Gibb is the former Vicar of St. Andrew's Church in Leyland and Honorary Canon of Blackburn Cathedral. He is committed to training church planters and gospel workers, and is one of the contributors to a new NIV Study Bible. He is also author of a book on Revelation.

Journey Through
Judges
by David Inrig

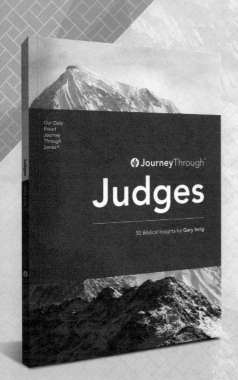

The book of Judges describes a low point in the history of God's people. It tells of a time of moral and spiritual anarchy, when everyone ignored God's life-giving laws and did what they thought was right in their own eyes. It is a story of disobedience and defeat. Yet the book also contains glimpses of the Israelites' capacity for greatness—when they chose to trust and depend on God. Discover God's great principles of life, and find out how we can lead powerful, productive lives in a society that is increasingly hostile to our faith.

Gary Inrig is a graduate of the University of British Columbia and Dallas Theological Seminary. An established Bible teacher and former pastor, he has authored several books, including *True North*, *The Parables*, *Forgiveness*, and *Whole Marriages in a Broken World*.

JourneyThrough
Matthew

Mike Raiter

JourneyThrough
Mark

Robert M. Solomon

JourneyThrough
Luke

Mike Raiter

JourneyThrough
John

David Cook

JourneyThrough
Acts

David Cook